Usborne Beginners
Under the sea

Fiona Patchett
Designed by Zoe Wray

Illustrated by Tetsuo Kushii and Zoe Wray

Consultant: Dr. Margaret Rostron

Reading consultant: Alison Kelly

Contents

Living underwater

Many amazing creatures live under the sea.
Some seas are warm and some are cold.
They can be deep, but some are shallow.

These bright fish live
in shallow seas.

Dolphins

Dolphins live in warm and cold seas.
They have smooth bodies which
help them to swim very fast.

Dolphins breathe through a hole on the
top of their head. It is called a blowhole.

A dolphin
swims to
the surface.

It breathes
out air. Water
sprays up.

It breathes
in and dives
underwater.

If a dolphin is sick, other dolphins take care of it.

A mother dolphin with two babies

A mother dolphin shows her baby how to breathe. She teaches it how to look for food.

5

Sharks

Sharks have many rows of sharp teeth.
They usually eat fish, squid or seals.

This is a great white shark.
It is the most dangerous
kind of shark.

How many rows of
teeth can you see?

This is a whale shark.
A whale shark is the
largest fish in the sea.

The fastest kind of shark
is the mako shark.

This hammerhead shark
has an eye at each end
of its wide head.

Some whale sharks are longer
than a bus!

Jellyfish

Jellyfish have no bones and no brains.
They look like blobs floating in the sea.
Some have tentacles that can sting.

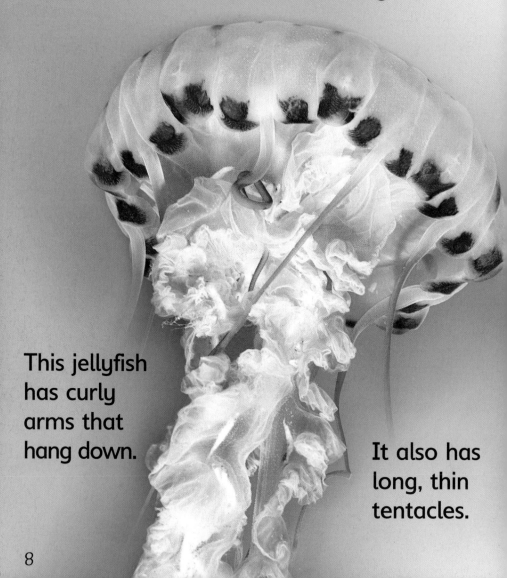

This jellyfish
has curly
arms that
hang down.

It also has
long, thin
tentacles.

A fish swims into the tentacles.

The tentacles sting the fish many times.

The arms push the fish into its mouth.

These are called upside-down jellyfish. They don't have long tentacles.

Some jellyfish have tentacles as long as a soccer field!

Flat fish

Some fish are flat. Some of them can change the shade of their skin to hide from other fish.

A plaice lies on a muddy sea bed. It looks like the mud.

It swims over sand. Its skin changes to look like the sand.

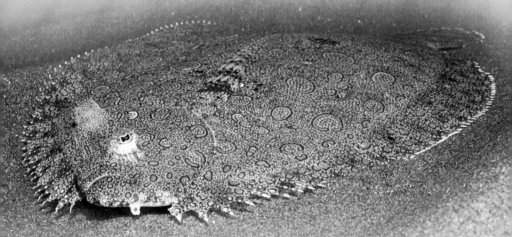

Most flat fish have both eyes on top of their body, like this peacock flounder.

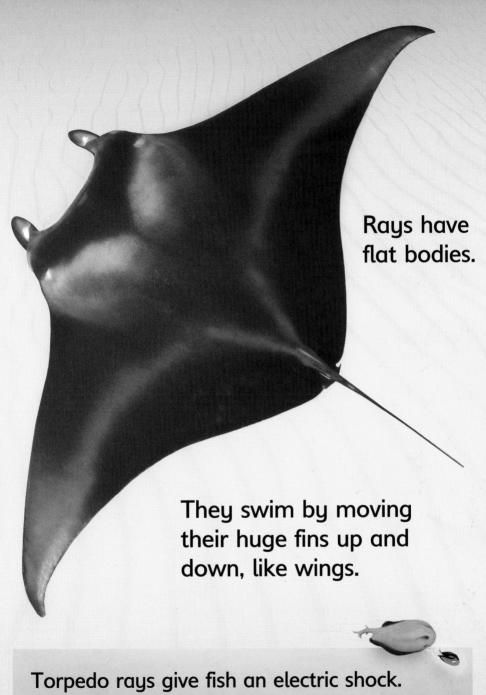

Rays have flat bodies.

They swim by moving their huge fins up and down, like wings.

Torpedo rays give fish an electric shock. Then they eat them.

Octopuses

Some sea creatures, such as eels, like to eat octopuses. When an octopus is scared, it hides in a cloud of ink.

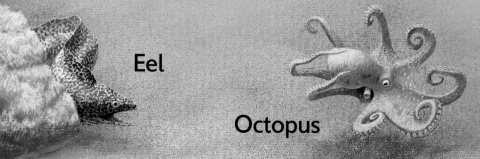

Eel

Octopus

The eel is waiting to attack the octopus.

The octopus sprays a cloud of ink at the eel.

The octopus moves away very fast.

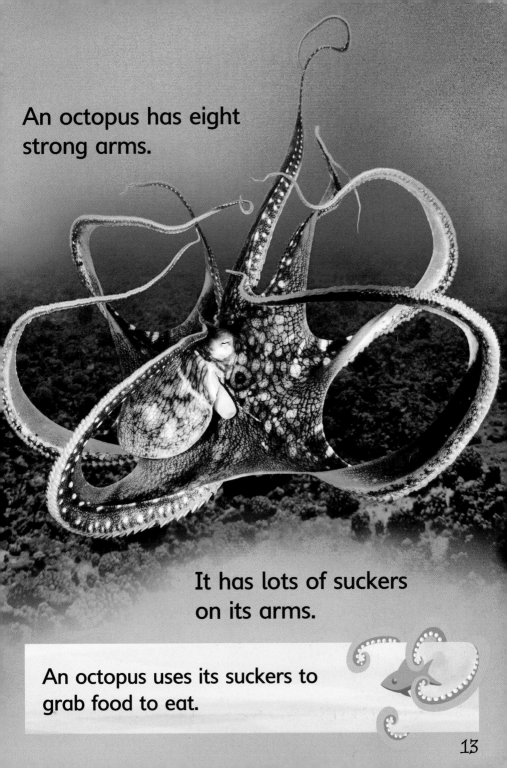

An octopus has eight strong arms.

It has lots of suckers on its arms.

An octopus uses its suckers to grab food to eat.

Sea turtles

Sea turtles live in warm seas. They lay their eggs on the land. They have a soft body which is protected by a hard shell.

This green sea turtle uses its flippers to swim through the water.

Sea turtles weigh about the same as adult human beings.

A sea turtle finds the beach where she was born to lay her own eggs.

She lays her eggs in a hole. She covers the eggs with sand. She goes back to the sea.

Baby turtles hatch out of the eggs. They find their way to the sea.

This sea turtle is hatching from its egg.

Dragons and horses

Dragons and horses live under the sea.
They are sea horses and sea dragons.

This is a leafy sea dragon. Parts
of its body are long and green.

Sea dragons can hide
easily because they look
like seaweed.

Sea horses are a kind of fish.

They swim upright.

They suck tiny animals through their mouths.

If a sea horse wants to stay in one place, it curls its tail around a sea plant.

17

Fast fish

Some fish can move very fast through the sea. They can even leap into the air.

These are flying fish. They can glide over the water for 45 seconds.

A flying fish uses its tail to swim faster.

It wiggles its tail. It leaps into the air.

It opens its fins and glides along.

This is a sailfish.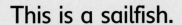

It has a spike above its mouth.
It is called a bill. It uses its
bill to attack fish to eat.

Sailfish are
the fastest
fish in the sea.

They can jump high
out of the water.

Sailfish have a huge fin on their back.
It looks like the sail of a boat.

Watch out!

Fish use clever tricks to scare other fish. Lionfish have long, poisonous spines. They flick them forward to scare other fish.

A lionfish

A shark has spotted a porcupinefish.

The porcupinefish swells up like a balloon.

It is too hard to eat. The shark swims away.

Some fish swim in a group, called a school.
Other fish may think the school is one big fish.

Penguins

Penguins dive into the sea to catch their food. They eat fish, squid and tiny sea animals.

These are rockhopper penguins. They dive from rocks or ice.

Penguins are birds, but they cannot fly. There are 17 kinds of penguins.

They leap out of the sea. They take a gulp of air and dive again.

Penguins swim very fast to catch their food.

23

Diving whales

Whales are the biggest animals in the sea.
Sperm whales dive deep down to find food.
They swim to the surface to breathe.

This is a sperm whale.
It can hold its breath
for over an hour
when it dives.

As a whale dives, it
throws its tail up.

This helps the whale
dive deeper.

Sperm whales eat squid. Some giant squid are as long as a whale.

Humpback whales swim near the surface of the water. They make noises that sound like songs. Nobody knows why.

Near the bottom

It is very dark and cold near the bottom of the sea. Strange fish live there. Lots of them have big mouths and sharp teeth.

Viper fish have very long teeth.

Angler fish have a light above their mouth. They eat fish that swim near.

Hatchet fish
have big eyes
on top of their head.

Gulper eels have
a huge mouth.

There isn't much to eat deep in the sea. Fish
wait for dead sea animals to sink from above.

Divers

Divers wear special clothes so they can swim under the water.

Fins

This tank contains air. It helps the diver breathe under the water.

Divers wear fins to help them swim.

Under the water, divers use their hands to tell other divers things.

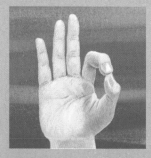
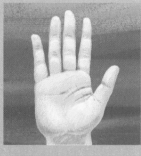

This sign means 'OK'.

This means 'stop', or 'wait'.

This means 'I'm going up'.

Some divers explore the wrecks of ships.

They may see old things, such as pots.

Some divers look at the plants and fish which live in the sea.

There are many shipwrecks under the sea which have never been found.

Glossary of undersea words

Here are some of the words in this book you might not know. This page tells you what they mean.

 blowhole - a hole on the top of a dolphin's head. It is used for breathing.

 tentacles - long parts of a jellyfish. They can sting.

 fins - parts of a fish. They help a fish swim. Divers wear plastic fins to help them swim.

 sucker - a round pad. It can stick to rocks and fish.

 poisonous - something poisonous can kill you. Some fish have poisonous spines.

 spines - sharp points which stick out of a fish's body.

Web sites to visit

If you have a computer, you can find out more about life under the sea on the Internet. On the Usborne Quicklinks Web site there are links to four fun Web sites.

Web site 1 - Print out pages of fish and sea animals to fill in and make into a book.

Web site 2 - Design your own fish.

Web site 3 - Find out more about whales.

Web site 4 - Try some sea slide-puzzle games.

To visit these Web sites, go to **www.usborne-quicklinks.com** and type the keywords "beginners sea". Then click on the link for the Web site you want to visit. Before you use the Internet, look at the safety guidelines inside the back cover of this book and ask an adult to read them with you.

Index

Acknowledgements

Managing editor: Fiona Watt, Managing designer: Mary Cartwright
With thanks to Mark Lazenby at PADI International Ltd.

Photo credits

The publishers are grateful to the following for permission to reproduce material. **Alamy:** 29
(Jan Wassmann). **Ardea London:** 8 (Ken Lucas), 24-25 (François Gohier). **Bruce Coleman:** 4
(Pacific Stock), 5 (Jeff Foott), 9 (Pacific Stock), 13 (Pacific Stock), 16 (Jim Watt), 18 (Kim Taylor),
19 (Pacific Stock). **Corbis:** 10 (Stephen Frink), 14 (Kennan Ward), 20 (Amos Nachoum).
Digital Vision: 2-3, 30-31, 32. **FLPA:** 15 (Iwago). **Natural History Photographic Agency:**
1 (B. Jones and M. Shimlock), 17 (Daniel Heuclin). **Oxford Scientific Films:** 11
(David B. Fleetham). **Still Pictures:** 6 (Kevin Aitken).

Every effort has been made to trace and acknowledge ownership of copyright. If any rights have
been omitted, the publishers offer to rectify this in any subsequent editions following notification.